DRUM SOLOS
THE ART OF PHRASING

by Colin Bailey
Author of BASS DRUM CONTROL

To access audio visit:
www.halleonard.com/mylibrary

6081-0764-7390-9615

ISBN 978-0-7935-9160-2

HAL•LEONARD®
7777 W. BLUEMOUND RD. P.O. BOX 13819 MILWAUKEE, WI 53213

Visit Hal Leonard Online at
www.halleonard.com

PREFACE

This book was written for Drummers with limited experience in playing Jazz music, and the kind of soloing it requires. I hope to give some insight into that idiom. I always solo in two or four bar phrases, as you will see in the written solos. This system can be carried on to play eight, twelve, sixteen bars, or however long the solo needs to be. It is much easier to think in terms of using the shorter phrases, two or four bars, and building on them, as opposed to thinking of a certain amount of bars as a whole. There needs to be organization in soloing in any kind of music. For example, if you have a solo or solos to play in a tune, it can't be just any disjointed assortment of beats, because it will not have continuity, and will lead to not coming out of the solo in the correct time frame. So, Drummers should solo in phrases, the same as other instrumentalists.

There are some methods for learning how to be comfortable with phrasing Drum solos. You may find it easier at first to start with one bar phrases. Just think of one bar at a time for playing a two or four bar solo. Play two bars of time on the ride cymbal before a two bar solo, and four bars of time before a 4 to feel the time of that number of bars. The next step is to think in two bar phrases. Put two 2's together and you have a 4, and so on to eight, twelve etc. As I said earlier, this is my approach to soloing, and eventually it will become natural for you to play solos in this form, as do most experienced Drummers. One very important thing for any instrumentalist is to have some stock phrases (licks !!), to help in creating solos. All good Jazz Drummers have this attribute, and can be recognized on recordings for their trademark styles. It is difficult to totally improvise solos without having some things to build around. I hope the material in this book will help you to get started with your own vocabulary. Listen to the recordings of the top Jazz Drummers and copy their solos, because listening to them is essential in learning this kind of playing.

On the audio, I play and solo with the Guitar and Bass on the first part, then you play and solo in the Drum solo spaces (with click - track). I hope that this book and audio will enlighten you to the concept of soloing in phrases.

PREFACE PART 2

TEMPOS

The tempos are whatever is comfortable. Most of the solos can be played at various speeds, and it will be obvious as to which tempo fits a certain solo. Memorize everything two bars at a time, as it is easier than reading everything all the time. Start slowly, and don't try to play any solo too fast before you are able to play it comfortably accurate.

STICKING

I have written suggested sticking where it is not an obvious R - L situation. These are the ones I use , to be able to play toms and cymbals in places that are different from the R - L system. It allows you to play more interesting rhythmic patterns. Also, when going back into time on the ride cymbal after a 4, 8, or whatever length solo has been played, it's usually with the right hand, so the sticking used should enable you to do that without any uncertainty. Of course, that is reversed for left handed Drummers! Ambidextrous Drummers are used to striking a cymbal with the left hand. So for them, it would depend on which hand they are going to use to go back into the time.

NOTATION

There is a great difference in metric time and syncopation. From a straight 1/8th feel to the triplet feel. There is often confusion in how to interpret the way a Drum chart is written, because sometimes you will see straight 1/8th notes or dotted 1/8th - 16/th combinations and they are both played with the same feel. Also, the way a cymbal time pattern is usually written. The second and fourth beats are either dotted 1/8th - 16th, or a triplet with a rest in the middle. The reason I mention this is because it applies to some of the solos in this book. I have mixed a few of these in so you can get accustomed to seeing such notation, and know what feel is usually played. On fast tempos, the 1/8th note groups would be played in a metric feel, because it would not sound right to play them in a syncopated way.

TIES

It's ok to play a solo with the last beat being tied over into the time bar that comes next. Then, the time on the ride cymbal would start on the second beat of that bar. It gives more options for the solos not to have to come back in on the first beat every time.

BUZZ - DRAG

I mention this because it is in a few of the solos. It's just as it looks. A buzz with one or both hands, as indicated. Not too tightly played.

WHOLE CHORUS SOLOING

The solo that many Drummers find difficult, is to play the entire chorus of a tune. To do this , you have to know the piece well and be able to hear it in your head and play your solo at the same time. It's like a form of independance. Band leaders will only let a Drummer take a solo chorus if they can trust him or her to come out of it in the correct place. There is nothing more uncomfortable for a band than not knowing where the Drummer is in a solo chorus.!!
There is a way to help learn how to do this. Play a standard or Jazz standard tune such as the three I have used as examples on pages 22 - 23 - 24. Play the melody, and fill in the spaces. This is the way I wrote the solos for those tunes. I call it melody soloing. It is a good idea to learn as much as you can of the standard repertoire used in Jazz, so that you can be familiar with a tune, and know where you are in the framework of it while you or others are soloing. The standards are played similarly as far as playing around the melody. For example, the first bar of Green Dolphin Street was originally written as a whole note, but is often played with two 1/8th notes, and three 1/4 notes rest. I used the whole note first bar in the example I wrote, so that the whole bar is a fill or solo. The second bar is utilizing the melody on the third and fourth beats, using the dotted 1/8th - 1/6th pattern, which was originally written as a quarter note triplet. Jazz players like to play around original melodies to syncopate it so that it swings. The way those songs were originally written were a little on the stiff side!!

FOUR BAR PHRASES THAT CROSS BAR LINES

They are continuos patterns of three beats that cross over the bar lines. It's good to learn how to get the feel of these, as they are fun to play and give solos a different approach. In a four bar solo, there is usually one beat left in the last bar after completing the cycle. In an eight bar solo, the cycle comes all the way around. I wrote twelve four bar examples of these phrases, and two different ways to play around them.

THE AUDIO

Playing with me on the audio are Bruce Forman, an internationally known Guitarist with many C.D.'s as a leader and with other prominent Jazz players. On String Bass is Scott Steed who has also played and recorded with many top musicians.
The five pieces we played were one standard, and four originals by Bruce Forman. We did tunes with various tempos, including one in 3/4, so that the soloing would be different on each one.
I transcribed my solos from the first part of the audio so that you can hear (and see) how I use phrasing. The second part is the PLAY - TO section, and has a Drum chart, and a solo chart. So, have fun and play along with those fine musicians.

FOOTNOTE

The solos in this book were not meant to be very technical. They are intended mainly to help in learning the two or four bar phrasing concept.

This will be the ledger line note set - up throughout the Book.

TWO BAR PHRASES

TWO BAR PHRASES

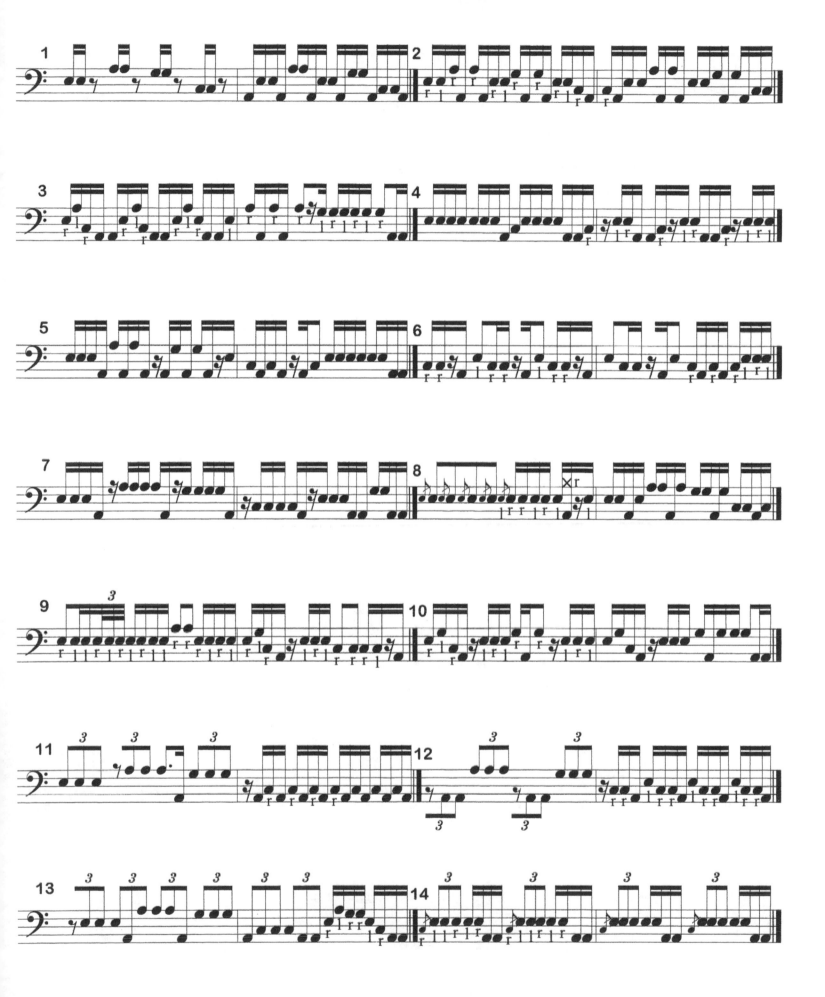

FOUR BAR SOLOS

FOUR BAR SOLOS

FOUR BAR SOLOS

FOUR BAR SOLOS

FOUR BAR SOLOS

tom rim - shots

FOUR BAR SOLOS

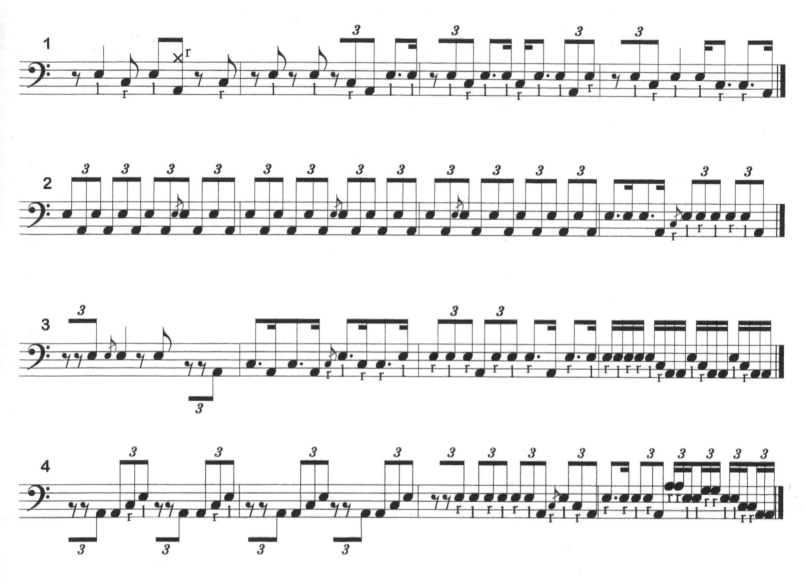

FOUR BAR SOLOS

15

FOUR BAR SOLOS (using Hi -Hat with Left Foot)

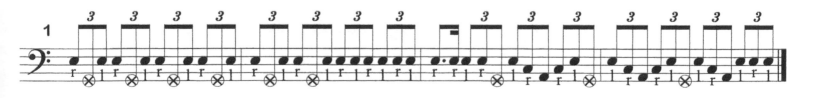

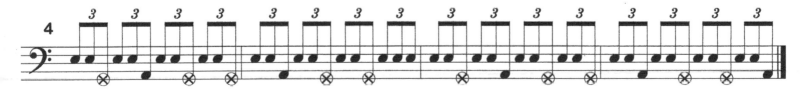

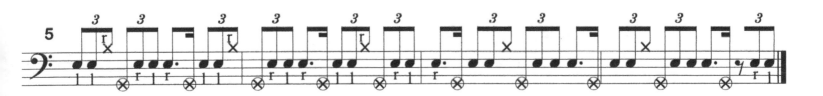

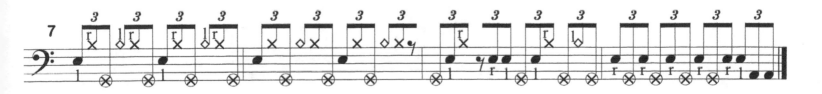

FOUR BAR SOLOS (using Hi-Hat with Left Foot)

FOUR BAR SOLOS IN 3/4

4 's In 3/4

EIGHT BAR SOLOS In 3/4

8's In 3/4

PARADIDDLES (around the set)

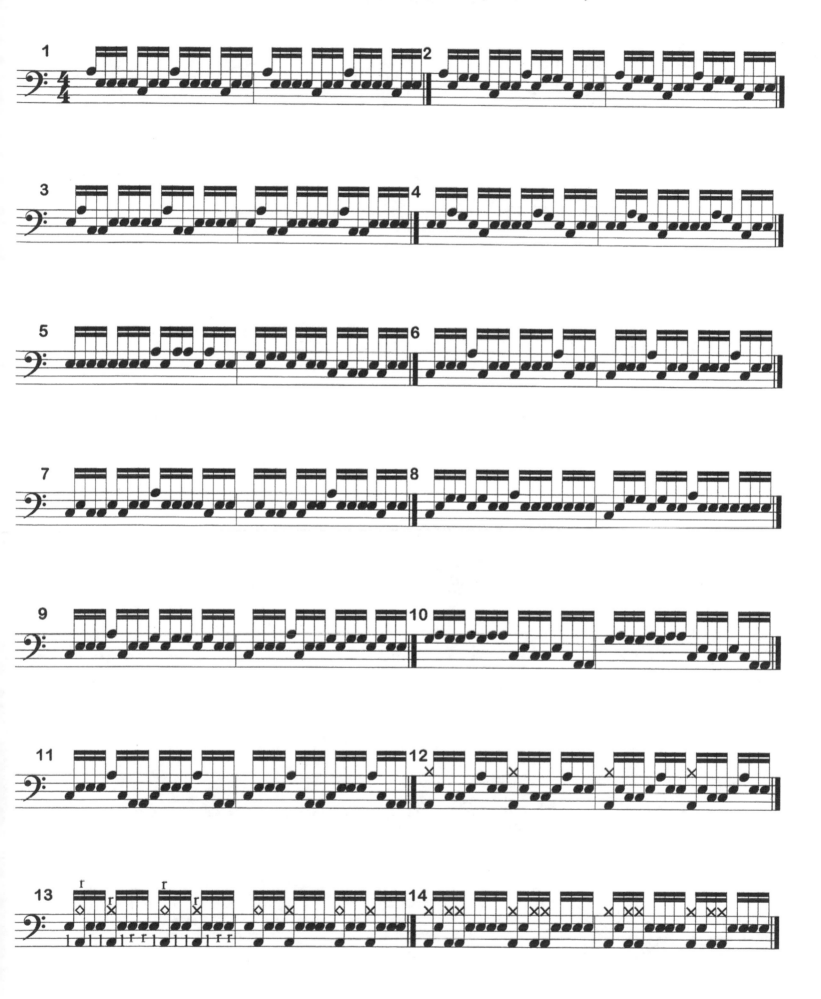

GREEN DOLPHIN STREET

Circled Notes Indicate Melody

STELLA BY STARLIGHT

Circled Notes Indicate Melody

AUTUMN LEAVES

Circled Notes Indicate Melody

FOUR BAR PHRASES That Cross Bar Lines

1

2

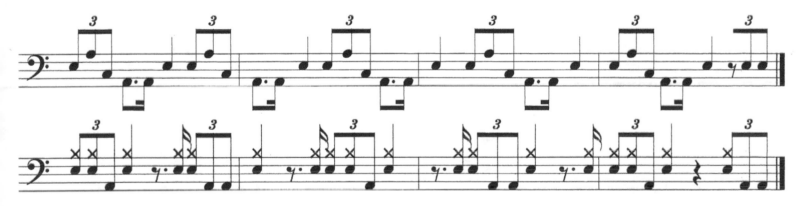

3

FOUR BAR PHRASES That Cross Bar Lines

FOUR BAR PHRASES That Cross Bar Lines

FOUR BAR PHRASES That Cross Bar Lines

Drum Chart No. 1   **I HEAR A RHAPSODY**   Fragos - Baker - Gasparre

I HEAR A RHAPSODY - SOLOS
One Chorus GUITAR - Two Choruses 4's
then last Chorus with Tag (on Drum Chart No.1)

I HEAR A RHAPSODY - Solos played on audio.

Drum Chart No. 2   **BLUESALIZER**   **Bruce Forman**

BLUESALIZER - SOLOS
Two Choruses GUITAR - Two Choruses 4's - One Chorus GUITAR - One Chorus DRUMS
go back to Drum Chart No.2 for last Chorus

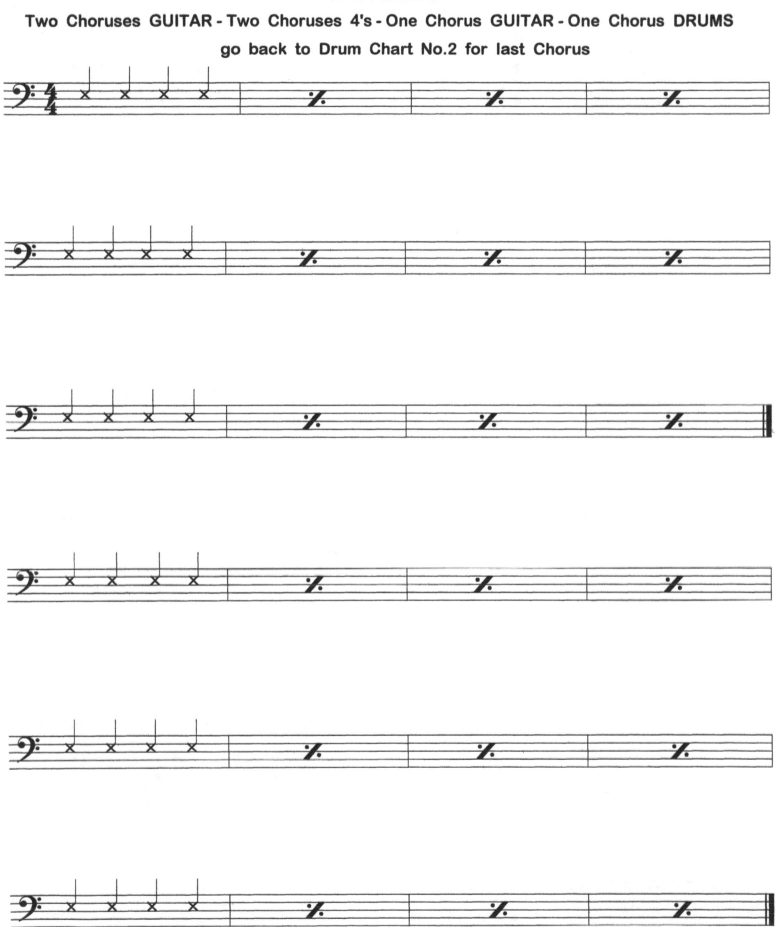

BLUESALIZER - Four Bar Solos

12 Bar Chorus

Drum Chart No. 3   **BOP SHOP**   **Bruce Forman**

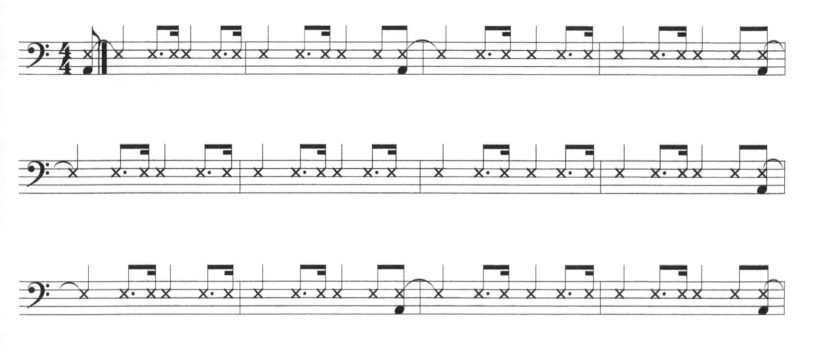

Bridge

cresc

cresc

End on last Chorus

BOP SHOP - SOLOS
One Chorus GUITAR - Two Choruses 4's - Two Choruses 8's
go back to Drum Chart No.3 for last chorus

Bridge

On last 8 bar Solo, catch the
last 8'th note back into Tune >

BOP SHOP - Four Bar Solos

BOP SHOP - Eight Bar Solos

Drum Chart No. 4   **CIRCULAR**   **Bruce Forman**

CIRCULAR - SOLOS
One Chorus GUITAR - One Chorus - 4's - One Chorus - 8's
go back to Drum Chart No.4 for last Chorus

after last Drum Solo 8

CIRCULAR - Four Bar Solos

Eight Bar Solos

Drum Chart No. 5

PRISIONE

Bruce Forman

PRISIONE - SOLOS
Two Choruses GUITAR - Two Choruses 8's
go back to Intro of Drum Chart No.5 for last Chorus

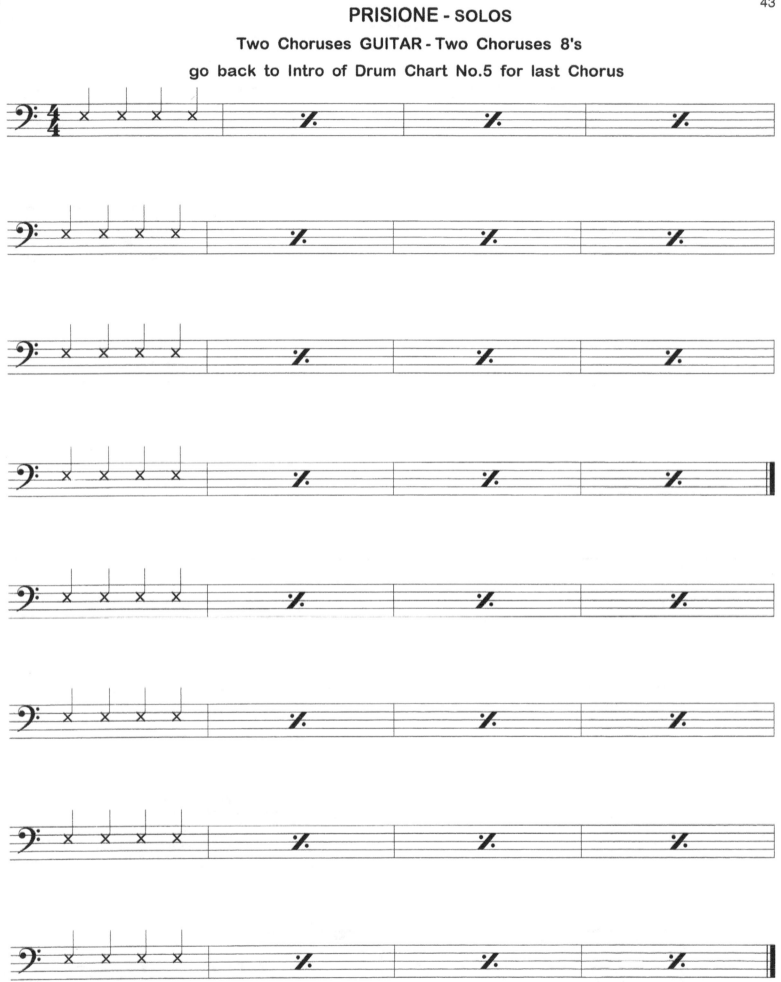

PRISIONE - Eight Bar Solos

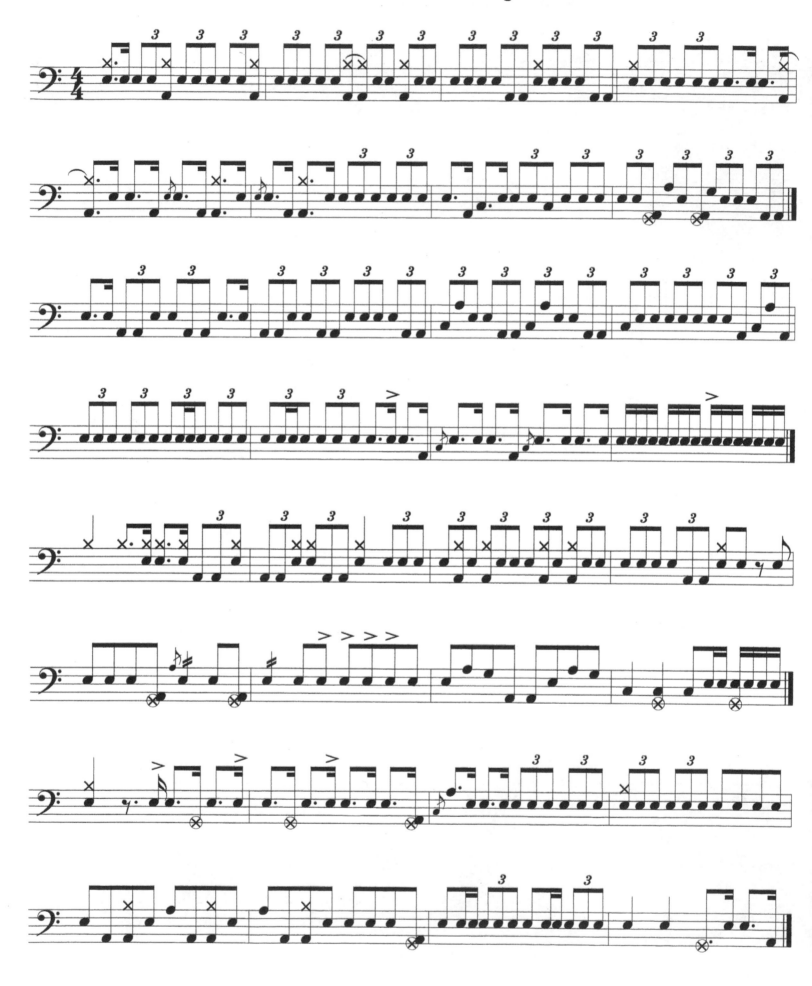